Up.

Down.

Sink.

Float.

This is a collection of poetry I have written over the years. The poems are raw, and are as diverse in location they were written as they are in emotion. Some were written on planes, some in grocery store aisles, and even in the shower. If you're my family or one of my close friends there's a good chance that you have heard one or a few of them. Either while floating down a river, sitting by a dying fire, sent over text, quietly reading at a bar or riding in the car under the streetlights, I've slowly let this side of me be seen. If I ever shared a poem with you and you asked me to repeat one, said it was good, asked me to send it to you, or honestly made any kind of remark at all, this book is here because of you. Thank you.

Up.

The languages, different.
The voices, the same.
My smile universal
When I say your name

You give me butterflies
Except they are caterpillars
Crawling all over
Turning the oddest bits
Into the most beautiful things
So wrap me into your cocoon,
I'm ready to fly, ready to swoon.

Here's to us,
And to this.
Here's to you, and I,
And bliss.

All I want
Is all your love
I'll lock my lips
And say when it's enough.

I'm a cloudy afternoon
She's a sunset sky
I'm last week's leftovers
And she's blueberry pie.

My affection
For you
Is growing.

Not sure
Where this
Is going.

I dive
Heart first
Not knowing.

Straight to
A waterfall
I'm rowing.

Throw a smile my way
Return a little nod,
We don't talk much,
But this is what we got.

You are stripes,
I'm polka dots.
When I close my eyes I see you
Instead of spots.

Please don't talk to me you said
I know you've been drinking
And a bit too honest you are
You blurt out what you're thinking.
Now you're holding the bottle.
I know exactly how you felt.
You pushed me away but now,
What you're saying makes me melt.

I get so high
When I'm with you
And sometimes we
Even do drugs too.

It's been a while
I had forgotten your smile.
But just like riding a bike
Seeing it made my day so bright.

We mesh so perfectly
Like we're heated in a kiln.
We always get along
Like two actors in a film.
When I'm with you
Everything is so easy.
Like the pizza that you eat,
I hope this ain't too cheesy.

Life is dark and dull
Full of things I don't know
You're a lightning bug.
I'm attached to your glow.

Many people make things more.
More things to say.
More things to be done.
More places I need to go.
But with you, everything is
Effort-less.

Everything came flooding back
with a single glance at your face.
I ran so far away, but one look,
and I'm standing back in place.

We used to sing separate songs.
Every hummed tune was different.
Then one day mine matched you.
And that's when I knew,
you are the melody
that was meant for me.

The higher the jump
The bigger the splash will be.
So I'm ready to risk
And feel the hurt if you leave.

I've found happiness.
Sometimes I look in your eyes
with a question on my face
and every time your answer is yes.

Relentless is your pull on me.
Like the moon on the tide and the Sea.
Waves constant, in rhythm and flow,
I am caught in your undertow.

If ever there's an ocean between us,
no matter the distance of the sea,
no matter the measure of time,
I'd sail through the storm,
just to see your coastline.

If I were a hunter,
then you'd be my prize.
I sit patiently through the night.
Seeing you, is like sunrise.

Threw away a moment,
the chance of a minute with you,
is worth more than an infinity of now.
I think you know who this is to.

Finally you're back,
I'm sorry if I vent
but it's easier to be true,
easier to be honest with you.

Whenever I let my words wonder
and let them grow free,
I notice they find their way to you.
And I guess my heart does too.

If your voice is music,
I'd turn up the volume.
If my ears ever bleed,
Your words are the cure.

We share a song
And it brings me back to you
Sing a little lyric
Thinking of you is all I'll do.

I'm playing my part.
Did you memorize your line?
I did.
Here's the part where I make you mine.

Everything is going wrong
I can count on you to keep me right.
Everything's coming loose
And it's you holding me tight.

I'll fly, I'll ride,
I'll walk, run or even swim.
If it makes you mine,
I'd crawl my way to you.

I think about you
More than I think about food
And I'm getting quite fat.
So I guess "love" would be my mood.

Grandma's been gone
For quite some time now.
But I still told her about you.

There's an open road in front of me
This time next year I don't know where I'll be
But I know where I want to go.
Anywhere with you I am fine
Any place I can call you mine.
I don't care where my feet are
If my hands hold yours, you hold my heart.

We contracted our friendship in writing.
We gave each other words as gifts.
We'd read between the lines.
We'd go off on tangents yet we'd rhyme.

When I rush into battle, I always bring my sword,
Like I plan to fight until the end.
When I rush into love, I always bring my S word,
Like *shit*, here it goes again.

Heart free like the pendulum in a grandfather clock
Brain thinking the same song that the cuckoo talks.
Eyes looking for you like a wrist missing it's watch.

We don't look before we leap.
Made our bed, and forced to sleep.
Jumped off the high dive, never learned to swim.
I guess we'll see if love works
When it's started on a whim.

Down.

I can't do this.
I can't push through.
All I think about,
Is you.

I should have known it was over
When you called me by the wrong name
That you had smelled a different rose
And you'd follow him wherever he goes.

I am an everlasting rain, falling for you and cannot stop.
I am a puddle in the storm, love overflowing with every drop.
Like a dam breaking down, you surely flood my mind.
If I'm a cyclone in the wind,
You're the sunshine not far behind.

I said it.
I can't take it back.
Stupid, dumb.
You'd say it to my face.
So I guess this time I'll just
Hold down backspace.

Falling for you was a journey.
Really quite the trip,
There were highs, and even more lows.
But now I'm home.
I'm back.
It's time to unpack.

I wasn't ready to stop talking.
I wasn't ready to stop listening.
I wasn't ready to be alone.
I can get along by myself, but
I had grown accustomed to the noise.
I had it droning in my ears.
I am not saying I loved it.
I was just distracted from my fears.

I can't stand being around you
It's all that I want to do.
I wish it weren't, but I know it's true.
And the worst is you don't want it too.

I think about you
A God damn, fucking awful lot.
I'm sorry for my language,
Lately it's all I've got.

It's funny how
I feel like I've lost you
And I'm more empty than
I ever was before,
But you were never mine.
There was never an us.
I'm just lost deep within myself
and loneliness.

The the train is derailed,
With wheels still turning.
The flame is snuffed,
But the coals stay warm.
The clock keeps ticking,
And the hands won't move.
Your love is taken, but I...
I'm still caught on you.

A long road
With a friend or two
It wasn't the plan but
I finally escaped you.

I'm forgetting about you
Like wind through the trees.
You once were my summer
But now I'm losing leaves.

We went digging for treasure
So obsessed with what we might find
That when we saw the chest tattered
We didn't care what was inside.

All you gave me was
Another smile to fake
Another band to hate
And a sweater I wish you didn't take.

I'm over you, you're not on my mind.
Other than late nights,
Or when I drive home,
I'm watching tv,
Or making dinner alone.

I never think about you.
Until I smell lavender,
Or warm cinnamon.
Read a funny article,
Or try to spell synonym.
(Did I get it right?)

Your name draws no feeling from me.
Well, that's if you don't count
Movies, books, or stories of any sort,
The nightly news, name tags,
Or announcements at the airport.

Yes, I'm doing fine without you.
Except for:
Always.

Someone asked me if I had somebody
I was surprised by your name on my lips.
I know that it's been a summer,
But sometimes it still slips.

Every time I see you, all you say is what we were.
One day the memories will fade, then where will you
find your words?

Getting over someone is much like a hill.
It's so difficult with the mud and dirt,
One tiny slip, and down you will slide,
Back at the bottom, a little more hurt.

I swore that never would I ever, take you back.
I told my friends.
Even told my family.
I told my coworkers,
I guess I never told me.

I grew to enjoy the feel of your arms
Pretty soon I'll grow out of it too.
Home changed to the sound of your voice.
Now anything else sounds brand new.

At last I'm finally free
There are no chains on me
I escaped from your spell
This feels like heaven,
I guess that makes you hell.

I am. Happy.
For you. For me.
Atleast, currently.
No telling what I seriously soon will be.

I make mistakes,
But don't let them burn.
I turn them into lessons.
From you, there's a lot I learned.

I wrote you a love letter
But now it's wasted ink.
You can throw it away,
It's no longer what I think.
At Least that's the way it seems,
It's no longer how I feel.
I guess it was a dream,
Cause you said it wasn't real.

Another late night,
Dark driving home,
No one else around,
Road all my own.
No music playing,
Just the rattle of the car,
You're long gone,
But I haven't got far.

Dreamt about you again last night.
So maybe, I'm not over you.
The trouble is, it's been a year. Or two.

I drank tonight,
And gave my brain the wheel,
It found its way to you.
We both know why I'm here.

Plenty of faces, none of them yours.
Plenty of hallways, but no open doors.

I'm waiting for a call
I know will never come
I don't want to admit it
But I know that we are done.

Once on the same path
Now we sail our ships separate
Both looking for treasure,
Maybe what you find
You will finally adore.

You thought you were the only one
She had a smile for,
Turns out someone else
Had that thought before.
Now you can't stand
Her smile anymore.

We're working toward what we want
Will you want me when you wake?

It rained and everything is soaked
Including my eyes
When it snows everything is white
Except for your lies.

I don't know why I'm caught up on you.
Trust me I would change it if I knew.
Is it your smile? Laugh? Walk?
Maybe it's how you make me feel,
But lately I'm not sure if that's real.

She's talking to me but I'm not hearing a single thing she's saying.
She's here with a change of clothes, I hope she knows she's not staying.

I should have seen it coming.
I'VE BEEN HURT LIKE THAT BEFORE.
She said that she should leave,
I RAN RIGHT OUT THE DOOR.
It's an easy choice to make,
SHE's DONE ALL THIS BEFORE.
I hope he loves you girl,
BECAUSE I DON'T ANYMORE.

We had passion and a flame,
We had the spark they talk about.
The fuse was lit, up we flew,
And just as fast the fire was out.

I hate admitting I was wrong,
But I'm here again like the chorus of a song.
So if the first verse is when I met you,
I think a key change is the only thing left to do.

I know it's been a year,
I still wish you were here.
I'm seeing you in my rear view mirror,
And you're the cause of most every tear.

He hoped she was happy.
And he really meant it.
He didn't regret their time together.
He'd just change how he spent it.

I know this pain might last long
Bye and bye, I'll be glad you're gone.

She told me that she's leaving,
That I had crossed the line.
I said I ain't believing,
You're lying like last time.

I came home today
And her things were all gone.
I missed the signs along the way,
And now she's moving on.

You.
You warm me up.
You pull me in.
You keep me coming back.
You're just like every addiction.
Today, I'm going sober.

Sink.

I just wish I could be one of those greats
You know the type.
I didn't need to describe it but you know.
You pictured something bigger than yourself.
So am I so wrong?

I'm a lonely man Been drifting to and fro'.
My heart hangs heavy And my mind is full.
But out here fishing, My soul is free.
Looking for a little catch and release.
Looking for a little catch and release.
I cast my line And I give in to hope.
Maybe this time she won't let go.
Maybe this time, but I know she won't.

Please let me not know
Please let me let go.
I'm looking through my own mind.
I'm scared of the things I might find.

One day I'll be happy. Right?
One day I'll make it?
One day I'll be alright?
And won't have to fake it?

If   I   were   to

Describe myself   in   four

Words   or   less,   then:

Wrong   place.   Wrong   time.

Banquet beside blood.
I feel I'm made of tin.
Hollow, heartbroken, hurt.
As if I had no kin.

I've been high.
I've been low.
It's difficult going down.
I thought you should know.

I fear the day when my thoughts learn to swim
And music can no longer
Drown them out
I fear the moment
When my reflection finds its voice
And tells me everything
That I don't want to know.
I fear the time
When I'll finally have to change
And won't accept the failure
That I've turned out to be.

If people read the things
That I say about myself
Then I bet they'd shut up
And put the book back on the shelf.

Dear Mom: I've been drinking
And I might just end it all tonight.
Dear Grandma: I've been thinking,
And I might come see you, if that's alright.
Dear sister: I've always loved you
And I'm sorry I haven't said it yet.
Dear brother: you're smarter in all you do.
I guess I'll never win that bet.
Dear Dad: I'm honest when I say I forgive.
I wish it hadn't changed a thing.
Dear me: turns out you won't get to live.
Life is a voice, you'll never get to sing.

Voices. They are liquid.
They move. They grow.
The more there are, the more I fall.
My silence sinks, with me in tow.

Thought about suicide.
Twice this week.
If suicide was hiding,
Then you could call me seek.

I can't seem to get my words straight.
Always saying the wrong thing.
Always at the wrong time.
I'm a vocalist with no lines to sing.

I'm drowning.
But I don't recall jumping in.
I'm choking
I don't remember breathing in.
I'm falling.
Never once did I fly.
I'm dying.
Did I ever feel alive?

Some people are loud.
Before they even speak.
Some personalities are oceans,
I'm a puddle with a leak.

Whoever said that
There's beauty in pain
Has never seen one try
To drown out their brain.

Creaking floors.
Squeaking doors.
This house is falling down.
Stumbling feet.
Restless sleep.
This life won't turn around.

I'm sitting in traffic
Living this life
Looking for an exit.
Reaching for the knife.
Glancing in the mirror,
Feeling so plain.
The world passes by,
I'm crawling the slow Lane.

The future is a debt collector.
If you reimburse on time,
Safe are your hopes and dreams.
But he's eating all of mine.

Voices are liquid.
Sometimes we drink.
Sometimes we sink.

I just want to throw the night away.
Grab a bottle, let my mind fade.
Fall in bed, crawl my way to sleep.
Expecting nightmares, hoping I don't dream.

I don't mean to rain on your parade
Wherever I go, clouds congregate.
I'm not trying to be something you hate
Happiness is a party, I'm running late.

You make me feel so small
Into myself I crawl.
I hide away, in plain sight.

I wake up,
It's still dark.
That's the way it goes
With a broken heart.
Pain thinks that it's not enough
Throws sorrow at me, And I wake up.
I drift back to sleep
On my own insecurity.

My heart is always in a race.
Running hard but seems,
To always come in last place.

Maybe I'm just scared.
Afraid to try again.
Loneliness is less painful,
Than losing a best friend.

I'm selling happiness,
The problem is, that it's mine.
I'm working my life away,
And running out of time.

Stay up late
Past the sunrise
Falling asleep
Tangerine skies.
I'm lonely again
Each and every day
So give me a bed
I'll sleep it all away.

Who are you?
A stranger asked,
Usually replied with name,
And reciprocated.
But the problem was
I did not know.
My identity? Just fuzz.

Lock me in a glass case
Listen to me scream
Distrust me when I say
That I'm not what I seem.
It's written on my face
You see it clear as day
That I'm a sinner and
You can't trust a thing I say.

Ever since I got a timepiece
I've been forced to face
My addiction to my cell phone
I used to play it off as
Oh I'm just checking the time
But while I'm here I might as well see
If anyone posted anything new
Did I get a text back?
What are they saying about me now?
So every time I lift my arm
And look at my wrist
I feel my fingers twitch
For that touch screen
And I watch the moments
Tick-Tock Tick-Tock
Time passing so slowly
Unlike your heart
When you're gripped by fear
And I'm focused on everywhere but here.

White lines guide him home
He gets where he wants to go
Either on the edge of the road
Or powder under his nose.

He loved her.
But never did he say.
And now he's haunted
By the words of yesterday.

Finally I felt strong enough
That maybe I could reach out
The time has come, much time has gone
I still say nothing. I'm the silent one.

Boom- Pop.
Gun- shot.
It takes months to make a life.
It takes moments to take a life.

I wash my hands of this mess.
I wash my mind of this stress.
I wash my soul of this sin,
But my heart knows where I've been.

I spend my energy on how I could do better
And everything I should have said.
If depression is an ocean,
My thoughts are made of lead.

The feelings have faded into memories.

The voices have vanished into echos.

The wound chose today as when to wake.

The emptiness at the far side of my bed breaks back into bleeding.

My mind turns to my chest pleading:

Please permit this to pass.

So I slumber still staying stuck.

My heart is locked away looking for a love that will lie.

She said you're such a great guy
You've really caught my eye
And I said you're no minister,
You haven't heard my sin,
What you see is shell
You don't know what's within.

The days went on
And on,
And on.
One day I'll be gone,
Gone,
Gone.

She said that she started writing.
Her pen was driven by what she read.
She needed to get the words out.
There was no room left in her head.

She said I was an inspiration.
I had sent her things that I had wrote.
But there is a vast difference,
From what she reads and what I note.

No,
I don't feel okay.
Oh
I've seen better days.
So,
I know it's just a phase.
Though,
I fear it's here to stay.

I guess I'm falling right back in .
I'll see you in hell 'cause I'm not forgiv'n.
Hello devil, here's my sin.

Some things bear more weight than one would think:
A bottle. A lifeless body.
A cigarette. A gun.
A new born child. A Bible.
A letter from your father.

Float.

I can get through this.
I will persevere.
Tomorrow when the smoke clears,
You'll see me standing here.

I may not be able to change my circumstance,
But I can change my stance in it.

I offered everything I was
But you said it wasn't enough.
Today I gave to someone else:
The diamond you found in the rough.

And speaking of jewels,
Do you miss wearing gold?
I guess you didn't know
What it was you got to hold.

When the sun refuses to rise,
I will forever shut my eyes.
I have no use for sight,
When the world is drenched in night.

I'm almost never bitter
But sometimes I bite.
Though, it's not who I am-
Swallowing people whole,
And it's hard to explain,
While ripping out a soul.

I turn up the music
And let it all out
Dance in the darkness
So only shadows hear me shout.

I wish there was a path
From my mind into yours
So my thoughts could go walking
Because I'm not good at talking.

In the story of life
You may not be the star
But you're the only one
That gets to write who you are.

Give me a road
And a car to drive with.
I'll sit there
In heavenly Bliss
Give me some asphalt
And space to ride
Just me. The concrete.
And adventures to find.
There's so much future
Toward where I can drive.
Possibilities plentiful
Where freedom can thrive.

Sometimes
Being alone
Sometimes
Feels like home.

I need a fresh wind
Something I can blow with
I need to catch my breath
And somewhere I can go sit.

I've never had a moment
That I'd consider defining
But I'm still hard at work,
It's me I'm refining.

Today I lit.
Today I flew.
Today I burned.
Today I blew.

I'm just struggling with
My own insecurities.
Trying to survive
and make it through my twenties.

Be the kind of person
That claps on a crowded Street,
Dances in the workplace
And won't let stress stop their feet.

When I laugh in the face of pain,
My smile is not fake.
When I joke surrounded in despair,
I do not hide behind comedy.
Hurt is deep, and I have felt my share.
Pretending it does not exist;
This is not my goal.
I've read that if you have a burn,
An affliction of the skin,
It's best to find the opposite.
Something cold and controlled.
Then take the pain, drive on in.

Home smells like the alfalfa field at the end of the street that I grew up on.

Home tastes like rusty water from a garden hose in the summer heat.

Home looks like a pair of headlights pulling into the driveway at 11:32pm as I wait eagerly on the porch.

Home sounds like my sister singing behind a closed door when she thought we didn't listen.

When I hug you, well home feels a little like you.

I'm just a dreamer
With my head in the clouds
Drifting in the sky
Hiding from the storms.

I'm plotting a course.
The only map I have is old advice
From broken people trying to stop me From making
their mistakes.
But no one has ever been where I am
And headed to where I'll go.
I'll have my own wrong doings.
I'll have my own chance to grow.

For once in my life
I don't know what to say
Because I don't feel threatened,
And the silence, well it can stay.

Turn and run.
My head said, go.
But my heart sat still.
Comfortable, planted to grow.

One hand on the wheel
Beneath the street lights
When I'm in this place
My mind wins the fights.

Remember this moment.
Remember this time.
Tomorrow when you wake up,
It might not rhyme.

When I fix something
I get the smallest idea that
Maybe,
The next thing is me.

When I listen closely
To every word you've said
I'm just relieved that this time
The voice isn't in my head.

I'll float with the river
Give way to time,
Yield to the rapids of life.
I have no rudder, no paddle, no ore.
I have faith that I'll make it,
Because I made it before.

There's something unexplainably comfortable
About having the ability to speak
And not needing to.

A broken heart, or too much on the mind
Know there is only one road to healing
Start up the car, drive to the weekend.
Needed is time for nature and kneeling.

Joy comes with effort
Pain from passivity
I work hard
To make my life easy.

Inhale the cold air, exhale stress.
I look at the lake, it calmly calls me to confess.
I slowly share my secrets and it sits so still.

I paddle upstream, determined.
I will reach my destination.
I cannot slow
Else succumb to the flow.

Improvement
Is less about getting where you're going
And more about being where you are.

I often translate my thoughts
Into words with ink,
It's usually the only way
To understand what I think.

I once dreamt I was drowning.
Gasping for air.
Choking on the water.
Clawing at the flowing fluid.
Being caressed by the current.
Sinking.
I awoke in a rage.
And slowly calmed my waves, fell silent and calm.
I cannot drown when I...
I am the sea.

Drown your misery in laughter
Subdue your sorrow with smiles.
Wash your anger in a soft voice,
And happiness will find its way home.

The path I choose is not always best,
But that's still okay.
You can follow me,
We'll get lost along the way.

I didn't find happiness.
It just kind of, happened.
I didn't one day wake up
With a smile on my face,
I struggled on my journey
Looking back,
I'm winning my race.

Advice to past me:
Hold on. Keep going.
You will succeed.
Advice from future me:
Watch out. Be careful.
Remember you can bleed.

I'm not looking for love,
I think I have it in me.
It comes from deep down,
I let it flow free.

In times of stress,
Silence shouts for me.
Solidarity holds me close
When I'm most lonely.
Depression may be a low,
But it's also my starting point.

Knowing your value
Is the key
For selling yourself
To someone that's worthy.

7A.M. cold snowy day.
Car hardly started,
Made it there anyway.
Driving too fast,
Slipping through the snow.
Walk down the stairs,
And what do you know:
So many faces, so many tears.
So many memories, everyone's here.
I kneel at your feet,
Though I can't feel mine.
You say, "I love you so much,
But your hands are so cold.
When I feel them I know,
That I'm getting old.
I'm glad I got to watch you grow."

Find me in the tall grass
Find me in the shade of the trees.
I drink from the river,
I rest by the stream.
Find me listening to songs,
Find there is no path I'm on.

I'm on my way up.
Sometimes I fall.
Nothing can stop me
Nothing at all.

Sometimes I fail.
Sometimes I fake it.
But I think,
I think I'm gonna make it.

Late night,
Meet up.
Just us,
Talk much.

The cold can nip at me,
Reach for me, bite at me
In any sort of way.
My deep warmth will
Carry me through the day.

Dance to the song
Inside my soul
The music: off beat,
But the melody: whole.
The notes are not known
By any definable key.
If it was given a name,
The title would be "Me."

Sway with the grass.
Breathe in the mist.
Sit in silence.
There find Bliss.

Breathe in.
Breathe out.
Exhale.
Don't forget to doubt.
This life is full of wonder.
One of these, you can live without.

Come on over
You don't have to knock
Walk right in
My door's never locked.

Never drag your feet
To help a friend
Never seal your lips
When asked for advice.
Always wear a smile
When loved ones tell a story.

Listen closer.
Talk quieter.
Take less.
Give more.
And love,
Will walk in the door.

It's fun to have everyone one around,
Happiness is easier when laughter
Is a common sound.

The crew keeps going,
Though we lost the captain.
The music is dead,
But the band keeps tapping.
Grandma's gone
And grandpa keeps granpin'.

Don't get off the bus
When it's not your stop
Ride it till the end
And end up on top.

Words of love drip from lips.
Swallow hate like hurricanes and ships.
Rage the seas, raise the tides.
When it comes to love, do not hide.

Let this balloon go
And float through the sky
Meeting new things
Learning to not be shy.

Be patient, I was told.
"You'll just have to wait"
But I pushed on forward,
And reached for my future.
I did not hesitate.

My soul is happy and full.
Who knew it was you?
Whom my depression had to pay the toll.

My life is on lease
Rent is due each day,
But the happier I am
The less I need to pay.

Just sit with me.
Just be close.
Just breathe the same air,
Just show me that you care.

To build a Utopia,
First you must learn
Don't lend a hand, give a hand,
And expect nothing in return.

Solitary is no curse
My voice unused
My comfort is so high.
Finally, the master of my mind.

The cold may make it
So my car won't start
But it won't affect
My warming heart.

Get the band back together
And play that song we do
Dance at different parts
Find the harmony, and move.

Hate like snow.
Let it fall slow.
Love like fire.
In this world it's dire.

Your happiness
And my happiness
Are not entwined.
If yours falls down
It won't affect mine.

I mumble my words,
When I try to talk.
But when I use ink,
The pen just walks.

We walk a path here, you and I.
Soon I know one of us will die.
The walk will continue, the path remains.
I'll still look for the places where your feet would
have lain.

Here am I existing
Happening and blissing.
The world is speaking
Here am I listening.

Treading lightly
Blazes no trail.
Success is nothing
With no risk to fail.

Give without thought of receipt.
Expecting something in return means
Your kindness is rooted in desciet.

"I'd like to see you again,
If that would be okay."
"Yes, absolutely.
I wish you said that yesterday."

You're sunshine rays
In a cloudy January.
You're gentle rain
In the heat of August.
You are a crackling fire
On an October night.
When trees bud in May,
You are their first light.

I don't know
what it is I'm praying for
But if you've got some God,
I could use a little more.
So give me some love, hope.
Give me strength, courage
Give me something
to make it through this day.

The days are getting longer
The sun is getting brighter
Here I am hoping
My sorrows will get lighter.

Happiness is like petrol;
Some people fill up and make it a long way,
Others stretch a gallon to make it through the day.

If you tell me who you are,
I'll tell you where I've been.
I know all the ups and downs of
All the town's that I've been in.

People are afraid to fly
They think they will die
But today I realized that
I'm not suicidal.
I bought airline tickets.

Don't do good things to be in heaven.
Do good things because heaven is in you.

Don't criticize a baby long,
For their cries could be your word for song.
How cruel to crawl the world about,
Only knowing how to shout.
Oh despair it would be to live,
With no words your emotions to give.

What you did is done,
What you do is up to you.

Write every sentence,
As if it is your last.
Read every book,
As if it is your first.
Listen as if words are water,
And all you are is thirst.

I've come so far
I made it through.
I don't know where I'd be,
Without you.

I said into the mirror,
To who I have become.
Because only I understand
Where I've come from.

The only thing
I'm out to prove
Is that I will
Improve.